Goldilocks and the Three Bears

Retold by Jenny Giles
Illustrated by Pat Reynolds

Once upon a time,
there were three bears.
They all lived together
in a house by a forest.

There was a great big father bear,
a middle-sized mother bear,
and a little baby bear.

Inside the house
there were three chairs.
There was a great big chair
for Father Bear.
There was a middle-sized chair
for Mother Bear, and there was
a little chair for Baby Bear.

Upstairs there were three beds.
There was a great big bed
for Father Bear.
There was a middle-sized bed
for Mother Bear, and there was
a little bed for Baby Bear.

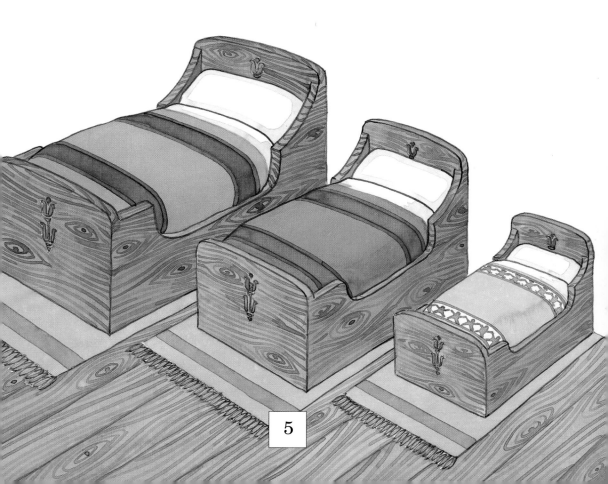

One morning,
Mother Bear made some porridge.
She put it into three bowls —
a great big bowl,
a middle-sized bowl,
and a little bowl.

"This porridge is too hot to eat!"
said Father Bear.

"Let's go for a walk while it cools,"
said Mother Bear.

"Let's go for a walk in the forest,"
said Baby Bear.

So off they all went.

While the three bears were out,
a little girl named Goldilocks
came to their house.

"I wonder who lives here,"
she said.
Goldilocks opened the door
and went inside.

Goldilocks went over to the table.
She tried the porridge
in the great big bowl.
"This porridge is too hot for me!"
she said.

She tried the porridge
in the middle-sized bowl.
"And **this** porridge is too hot for me!"
she said.

Then Goldilocks tried the porridge
in the little bowl.
"**This** porridge is just right!"
she said.

And she ate it all up.

Goldilocks went over to the chairs.
She tried the great big chair.
"This chair is too big for me!"
she said.

She tried the middle-sized chair.
"And **this** chair is too big for me!"
she said.

Then Goldilocks tried
the little chair.
"**This** chair is just right!" she said.

So Goldilocks sat down
in Baby Bear's chair —
and it broke!

Then Goldilocks went upstairs.
She tried the great big bed.
"This bed is too high for me!"
she said.

She tried the middle-sized bed.
"And **this** bed is too high for me!"
she said.

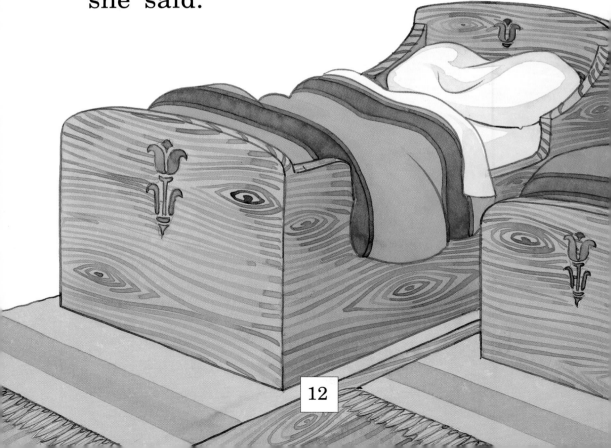

Then Goldilocks tried
the little bed.
"**This** bed is just right!" she said.

Goldilocks laid down
in Baby Bear's bed,
and soon she was fast asleep.

After a while,
the three bears came home.
They looked at their porridge.

Father Bear said,
"Someone's been eating **my** porridge!"

Mother Bear said,
"Someone's been eating **my** porridge!"

"Look!" said Baby Bear.
"Someone's been eating **my** porridge,
and it's all gone!"

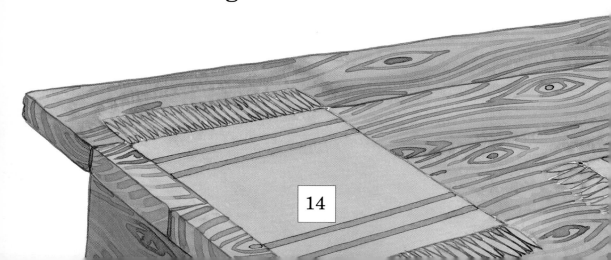

The three bears looked at their chairs.

Father Bear said,
"Someone's been sitting on **my** chair!"

Mother Bear said,
"Someone's been sitting on **my** chair!"

"Look!" said Baby Bear.
"Someone's been sitting on **my** chair,
and it's all broken!"

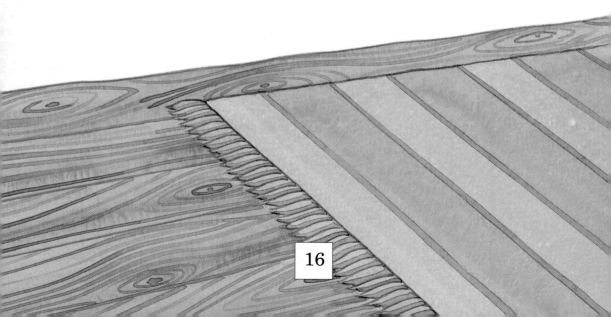

17

Then the three bears went upstairs.

Father Bear said,
"Someone's been sleeping in **my** bed!"

Mother Bear said,
"Someone's been sleeping in **my** bed!"

"Look!" said Baby Bear.
"Someone's been sleeping
in **my** bed...
and here she is!"

Goldilocks woke up
and saw the three bears
looking at her.
She jumped out
of Baby Bear's bed,
and ran out of the house
as fast as she could go.

Goldilocks ran all the way home,
and the three bears
never saw her again.

A play

Goldilocks and the Three Bears

People in the play

 Narrator

 Mother Bear

 Goldilocks

 Baby Bear

 Father Bear

Narrator

Once upon a time,
there were three bears.
They all lived together
in a house by a forest.
There was a great big father bear,
a middle-sized mother bear,
and a little baby bear.

Father Bear

I'm Father Bear, and I sit
in this great big chair.

Mother Bear

I'm Mother Bear, and I sit
in this middle-sized chair.

Baby Bear

I'm Baby Bear, and I sit
in this little chair.

Narrator

Upstairs there were three beds.

Father Bear

I sleep in the great big bed.

Mother Bear

I sleep in the middle-sized bed.

Baby Bear

And I sleep in the little bed.

Narrator

One morning,
Mother Bear made some porridge.
She put it into three bowls.

Father Bear

I have the great big bowl
of porridge.

Mother Bear

I have the middle-sized bowl
of porridge.

Baby Bear

I have the little bowl of porridge.

Father Bear

This porridge is too hot to eat!

Mother Bear

Let's go for a walk while it cools.

Baby Bear

Let's go for a walk in the forest.

Narrator

While the three bears were out,
a little girl named Goldilocks
came to their house.

Goldilocks

I wonder who lives here...
I think I'll go inside.

Narrator

Goldilocks went over to the table.
She tried the porridge
in the great big bowl.

Goldilocks

This porridge is too hot for me!

Narrator

Goldilocks tried the porridge
in the middle-sized bowl.

Goldilocks

And **this** porridge is too hot for me!

Narrator

Then Goldilocks tried the porridge
in the little bowl.

Goldilocks

This porridge is just right!
I'm going to eat it all up.

Narrator

Goldilocks went over to the chairs.
She tried the great big chair.

Goldilocks

This chair is too big for me!

Narrator

Goldilocks tried
the middle-sized chair.

Goldilocks

And **this** chair is too big for me!

Narrator

Then Goldilocks tried
the little chair.

...s

...ir is just right!

...g to sit in it.

...I've broken it!

Narrator

Then Goldilocks went upstairs.
She tried the great big bed.

Goldilocks

This bed is too high for me!

Narrator

Goldilocks tried the middle-sized bed.

Goldilocks

And **this** bed is too high for me!

Narrator

Then Goldilocks tried
the little bed.

Goldilocks

This bed is just right!
I'm going to lay down on it.

Narrator

Goldilocks laid down
in Baby Bear's bed,
and soon she was fast asleep.
After a while,
the three bears came home.
They looked at their porridge.

Father Bear

Someone's been eating **my** porridge!

Mother Bear

Someone's been eating **my** porridge!

Baby Bear

Look! Someone's been eating **my** porridge, and it's all gone!

Narrator

The three bears
looked at their chairs.

Father Bear

Someone's been sitting on **my** chair!

Mother Bear

Someone's been sitting on **my** chair!

Baby Bear

Look! Someone's been sitting
on **my** chair, and it's all broken!

Narrator

Then the three bears went upstairs.
They looked at their beds.

Father Bear

Someone's been sleeping in **my** bed!

Mother Bear

Someone's been sleeping in **my** bed!

Baby Bear

Look! Someone's been sleeping
in **my** bed...
and here she is!

Goldilocks

Oh! **Oh! OH!**

Narrator

Goldilocks jumped out
of Baby Bear's bed,
and ran out of the house
as fast as she could go.
Then she ran all the way home,
and the three bears
never saw Goldilocks again.